The Blue Squirrel

By Linda Nelson

Published by: Book Writing Founders
www.bookwritingfounders.com

Book Writing Founders
Your Dream-Published

This book is dedicated to my grandchildren:

Taylor, Joseph, Holden, Ava, and Austin
whom I love very much

The weather was getting warm, and more and more people were coming out to enjoy the sunshine. Even in my little community everyone was gathering to find out the news of the day. There seemed to be a great deal of talk about a newcomer, his name was Gus. He came from across town and was not happy with the quietness he was experiencing and limited space he was being offered. There was much talking and getting acquainted meeting with the other squirrels. Gus was not terribly happy with the new surroundings but seems to be talking and laughing with everybody and fitting right in. The squirrels were telling Gus that during the summer the college campus is fairly quiet but come September the students are back and sometimes it's hard to get across the yard.

Gus was all ears when he heard about the students and what happens on the campus in the fall. He could hardly wait until September. The squirrels told Gus that the students are friendly and usually leave crumbs and goodies for them to eat. This made Gus very happy indeed, and his attitude was changing about living in cramped conditions on a college campus. The next day, Gus met all the squirrels.

Freddie

There were so many of them that he could not remember all their names. The first to make his acquaintance was Freddie, known to everyone as "the pest". Then came Rocky, known as the "peace maker".

Rocky

Cly

Then there was Clyde "the know it all" and the best of all, Patty, the prettiest one of them all. Gus had never seen a more beautiful squirrel.

Patty

He immediately decided to ask Patty to come with him for lunch and she accepted. She was so easy to talk to. They would spend many days just happy being together. Patty told Gus about the other squirrels and especially about Freddie. He was always in everybody's business. Patty told Gus to try and stay out of his way and not to tell him anything he did not want to be repeated. Rocky was the tough guy in the group and was always ready to fight. Patty told Gus to stay on his good side. You never know when you might need a big strong friend in the community. Gus just laughed. Then she told Gus about Clyde, who knew every inch of the campus and everyone on it. Patty told Gus, "If you need something, just ask Clyde."

During the summer, the squirrels like to make up different types of games to keep them busy, Patty told Gus. Since Gus was the newcomer, the squirrels decided to let him be the one to pick what type of game they could play. Gus was happy they chose him for this task and sat thinking for a while. This made Freddie nervous and he kept running up and down the tree until finally Gus was ready. Gus decided it would be fun to see who could gather the most nuts and bring them to his house where they would be counted. The winner would get a meal made for him by Patty. She was a wonderful cook. The squirrels thought about this for a minute, realizing this would be difficult since it was summer and nuts were not easily available. Finally, everyone agreed and quickly took their places on the starting line. Gus told the squirrels he would give them one hour to gather the nuts and bring them to his home. Gus and Patty sat and watched the squirrels running here and there trying to gather enough nuts to win a home cooked meal from Patty. While they were together Gus and Patty were deciding on what she should make for the winner. Gus was happy he and Patty were such good friends. She reminded Gus about the time, and quickly Gus stood up and made a large noise and all the squirrels stopped and looked up. They knew the time was up. All the squirrels were outside of Gus 's home in minutes. There were quite a number of nuts, to everyone's surprise. Gus proceeded to count them up. After some time, the winner was announced. It was Freddie. All the squirrels applauded him and asked him how he found so many nuts?

He told them he had stored extra in the fall just to have ready in case he was really really hungry. Gus and Patty took the large red ribbon from the box and placed it around Freddie's neck. You could see how proud he was. When all the nuts were picked up and put away. Gus and Patty and Freddie started to walk to Patty's home for that wonderful dinner. On the way, Freddie asked what were they having. Patty told him it was a surprise. All she would say was that dessert was homemade ice cream. That was Freddie's favorite food so the meal really was not important. During the days that followed, Gus seemed to be having trouble with Freddie. He was always making up stories about Gus and telling them to Patty. Freddie and Patty were friends before Gus came to live on campus but they were never the kind of friends that Gus and Patty had become. Sometimes, it was even hard for Patty not to believe Freddie's stories, as they were so real sounding. Patty would have to ask Gus and this would make him mad. He told Patty that whatever Freddie tells you, just ignore it. She told Gus she would not pay attention to any more stories. Gus decided to speak with Freddie himself to make sure he did not make up any more stories about him. He was walking down the path that leads to the cafeteria when he spotted him. "Hi" he said. "What's up?" "Not much." Gus answered. I just thought it was time you and I had a little talk. Freddie just stared at Gus. "I am fed up with those stories you keep telling Patty about me that are not true. I want you to stop now and never tell another story about me again. Freddie looked into Gus's eyes and knew that he was not kidding. "O.K.", he said but somehow, he did not believe him. All the squirrels that lived on the college campus were from many different parts of the world and they got along just great. During the late summer evenings Gus would have all the squirrels together and one by one each one would tell a story of where he or she came from and what his country was like. Some of the squirrels told great stories and Gus just loved those summer evenings. The stories were so interesting you would feel as if you had been there too. Some of the squirrels came from China, Columbia, Korea, Ireland, Spain, U.S.A., Alaska and even Hawaii. The squirrel 's learned about the different types of food from their countries and even the different ways they communicated.

Everyone looked forward to these meetings and Patty and Gus would learn more and more about each other. When these meetings ended, everyone was calmer and ready for a good night's sleep. One day while Gus was walking on campus, he noticed a pretty girl sitting under his tree with a large dog. She was reading and eating an apple. This was the first student he had seen and wanted to get to know her before classes started. He was undecided how to go about this task. He remembered being told by the squirrels that the students were friendly, but he was still not sure, what to do. He had wished that Patty was there to help him out but decided he would be better doing this alone. He walked slowly, getting closer and closer to the girl. He was surprised to notice that neither she nor the dog moved. He guessed it was because he was being as quiet as possible. Just as he reached the girl she moved and nearly fell over on him. The dog got up and seemed to wait for the girl to tell him what to do. They seemed to be so happy together and it was as if both knew exactly what the other was going to do. Gus decided not to try this meeting today. It would have to wait. Just as he was about to leave, the girl got comfortable again and the dog sat down. Gus decided to stay and try again. He went closer to the girl and pushed against her dress. She moved and said "What was that?" her hand feeling for the grass beneath her blanket. Gus was surprised she did not try and speak to him.

slowly, getting closer and closer to the girl. He was surprised to notice that neither she nor the dog moved. He guessed it was because he was being as quiet as possible. Just as he reached the girl she moved and nearly fell over on him. The dog got up and seemed to wait for the girl to tell him what to do. They seemed to be so happy together and it was as if both knew exactly what the other was going to do. Gus decided not to try this meeting today. It would have to wait. Just as he was about to leave, the girl got comfortable again and the dog sat down. Gus decided to stay and try again. He went closer to the girl and pushed against her dress. She moved and said "What was that?" her hand feeling for the grass beneath her blanket. Gus was surprised she did not try and speak to him.

He did not want to scare her. How was he going to get her attention and her dog by not making her run away. He thought for a minute, and then stood up as quietly as he could and started to make some noise. The dog started to bark and the girl jumped up. Gus ran up the tree and waited. The girl and her dog walked away. Gus was very sad. There was something special about the girl and her dog. Gus decided to stop by and see Patty and tell her about the girl and her

dog maybe she knew her. Gus was right Patty and the other squirrels did know her. Her name was Joy and her dog's name was Hero. Patty told Gus that Joy was blind and that her dog Hero was given to her a long time ago to make her feel better and make sure he would take good care of her always. Hero knows how to make sure Joy gets from one place to another. He is a trained seeing eye dog. Hero sleeps with Joy in the same room and when Joy needs to go out Hero is always with her.Patty told Gus if he wanted to meet Joy and Hero she could arrange for that to happen. Gus was so excited that Patty could do this for him. The very next day Patty and Gus walked to the part of the campus where she knew Joy and Hero would be. It was the cafeteria.

Gus was getting nervous but Patty told him to be calm. Just then Joy and Hero came along. Patty called out to Joy and Hero, they both stopped. Patty introduced Gus to Joy and Hero. Gus told Joy that he wanted to meet them the day they were sitting under the big oak tree but was afraid. Joy told Gus that she and Hero were so happy to meet a new friend. They decided to go and sit under the big oak tree and talk. Gus, Patty, Hero, and Joy had a wonderful day talking and laughing together.

They would do it again very soon. That evening, Gus told everyone to come over to his house to watch a movie and to bring some popcorn. He liked to entertain and he also enjoyed having all the friends together. After the movie there was laughter and joking. When it was time to go, everyone told Gus what a wonderful time they had and that they should do it again soon. He agreed and told Patty how wonderful it was having a friend like her. Patty told Gus she had to get up early the next morning and would like to go home now. The evening was clear and comfortable. Classes would be starting in a few days and Gus was excited about this. After leaving her he decided to take the long way home. On the way, he was thinking about Patty and how much he liked it here and about his new friends

Joy and Hero. He was also thinking about how happy he was that he came to live on campus and how all the squirrels got along so well even though they were all so different. Yet he knew deep down they were really all the same. As he was

passing by the campus fountain he noticed Freddie, Clyde and Rocky trying to catch the lizards that live around the fountain

Gus watched them for a while and realized he was up for a little mischief himself, so he decided to join them. They were happy to see him, but when they couldn't find any lizards to play with they said it was time to go home. Gus decided to cut through the freshmen fence as it was the quicker way home and he was tired. Freddie was trying to chase a bird from the tree and making a terrible racket. Gus just Ignored it and stayed in bed a little longer. He did not sleep well the night before and he had to meet Patty for their afternoon walk around the campus. He didn't feel up to walking especially in the rain. He was hoping that Patty would want to stay home and just relax. This was not likely with her, she always wanted to find something different to do. As he peeked out of his tree he no– ticed that the rain was stopping. He got dressed and made his way down the tree. As he walked to Patty's house, he noticed a large group of students at the fountain in the middle of the campus. They were trying to decide on a blue color of paint for the fence outside the freshmen dorm. It was tradition for each new class to change the color of the fence so that everyone knew who the freshmen were.

Gus wanted to watch them do this, but realized that Patty was waiting. He hurried to get her and then they both returned to the activity on campus. They waited until the fence

was finished and then decided to try and search some ice cream or cookie crumbs left behind by the students.

Freddie found Patty and Gus and started teasing Gus about the color of the new fence and this made Patty angry so they decided to just leave. On the way back to Patty 's house Gus told her even though Freddie was annoying she should try and get along with him after all they were all neighbors. Patty agreed. Morning came sooner than Gus expect– ed. He had slept well and the sun was shinning brightly. He jumped up from bed, made a quick breakfast, and then went off to meet friends and hear about the news of the day. When Gus met up with his friends, they had a strange look about them. Some of them were even laughing and they would not tell him why. He was getting angry with them because he felt they were laughing at him for no reason. Freddie came close to him and started laughing uncontrollably. At this, Gus became extremely upset and just ran away. He ran to his tree and just sat there until he could catch his breath and find out what was so funny. Since most of the squirrels were always making jokes, he decided to forget about it. He then went to see Patty, but she was not at home yet. While Gus was walking around the campus, he noticed that students were pointing to him and laughing. First his friends, and now the students. This had never happened to him before. What was so funny? He tried to get to Patty 's house again but every time he passed a student they would laugh uncontrollably. He quickly returned to his tree where Joy and Hero were relaxing. He was safe. "Hi Joy," he said. Joy turned toward him and noticed that he was completely out of breath. She told him to lie down next to her and Hero and just relax. Gus felt safe and fell fast asleep. When

Gus awoke, Joy and Hero had gone. He felt alone again and scared. He ran up his tree and decided to stay inside for a while so no one could make fun of him. After a short while he decided to go out again. When he reached the bottom of the tree, he noticed a piece of broken mirror. When he picked up the mirror, he looked into it and noticed that he was painted BLUE, he was too numb to speak or move.

How could this have happened? No wonder everybody was laughing at him and no one would tell him what was the matter. Then he remembered. The night before, when he had stopped by the fountain to play with Clyde, Freddie and Rocky, he had slipped under the new freshman fence. It was probably not dry when he went through. Gus thought, "I should get to Patty 's house as fast as I can, she will know what to do for me." When he arrived, she opened the door and just stood there with her mouth open. She would not let him in. He could not believe what was happening. It wasn 't his fault that he was BLUE. Why didn 't Patty try and help him instead of closing the door on him? He was so ashamed of having been so foolish. He made his way back across the quad on campus and by now the whole campus knew about the BLUE squirrel. He was the laughing stock of the neighborhood. He just did not know what to do. The only thing left to do was to leave this pleasant community, his friends and home behind. He thought, "No one wants to be with me anyway. Everyone has turned against me just because I am blue now. Inside I am still the same old Gus. Wasn't this good enough for them? He wondered how they would feel if they were all different someday. How would they feel about that? As he walked by the familiar buildings on campus for the last time, he could see his tree in the distance. He thought Joy and Hero might be there but quickly remembered it was Saturday and she did not come on the weekends. He looked up at the sky and it was gray with thickening clouds. It was going to rain: he had to hurry or get drenched. He could not have felt any worse, or looked any sillier. When he reached his tree, he was soaked to the bone. He ran up into bed as fast as he could, thinking tomorrow would be a better day. The next day wasn't any better than the day before. He started to pack for his trip and kept back the tears. As he gave his home one last look and made his way down the tree, he noticed a figure standing at the bottom. It was Patty! He was so happy to see her. She told him she had

something to say but she was waiting for the others. He had no idea why all the other squir- rels had to be by his tree. Having Patty there was embarrassment enough. Since it was still raining slightly, Patty and the others had their raincoats on and he wished he had bought one when he had the chance but he didn't.

Just then, the squirrels arrived and Patty told them to remove their raincoats along with hers. He could not believe his eyes. Everyone was painted a different color. They looked like a huge rainbow. It was beautiful. Patty said, "the squirrels wanted to apologize for laughing at you so they painted themselves to be like you." Gus was too shocked to speak. They asked him to stay. He told them he never wanted to leave. Patty looked great as a pink squirrel. He would love her no matter what color she was. Just then Patty, looked at Gus and started to laugh again. He could not understand this. She handed him a mirror and told him to look into it. He started jumping up and down. He was no longer blue as the rain washed away the paint. Now everybody started laughing, and hoping it would rain again soon. That was the happiest day of his life. They all learned a very valuable lesson from this. Gus was so happy to have Patty back and all the squirrels were together again. Nothing would every change that.

Everyone learned a lesson from what happened to Gus and how respect is so import– ant in every way. The respect to teachers, parents, friends and others makes everyone feel so wanted and loved. Gus was so happy to be with his friends again and knew how much they really love him and he loves them.

The End

About the Author

Linda Nelson lives on the East End of Long Island, New York and is a graduate of Chamberlayne College in Massachusetts. She has written articles about animals and their behavior in a fictional form for some time. Her inspiration for this book was her love of children and the pleasure that reading brings to a young audience. This Blue Squirrel brings you directly into the adventures of its main character Gus whom you learn to admire and want to read more about. Presently another sequel is being worked on and hope to be completed by years end.

... More to read from Linda Nelson

Find it on Amazon

www.ingramcontent.com/pod-product-compliance
Ingram Content Group UK Ltd.
Pitfield, Milton Keynes, MK11 3LW, UK
UKHW061031310726
14089UKWH00009B/199